Bella Goodrich

STARS

STARS

SEYMOUR SIMON

MORROW JUNIOR BOOKS
New York

To Joyce

PHOTO CREDITS
Association of Universities for Research in Astronomy, page 32;
Kyle Cudworth, The Yerkes Observatory, pages 5, 7;
Jet Propulsion Laboratory, pages 26, 29;
NASA, pages 12, 17, 19, 21, 22, 24; and
National Optical Astronomy Observatories, pages 2, 8, 11, 15, 16, 30.

William Morrow and Company, Inc.,
1350 Avenue of the Americas,
New York, NY 10019.
Printed in Mexico
7 8 9 10

Library of Congress Cataloging-in-Publication Data
Simon, Seymour.
Stars.
Summary: Discusses the stars, their composition, and
characteristics with actual photographs.
1. Stars—Juvenile literature.   [1. Stars]
I. Title.
QB801.7.S56 1986   523.8   85-32012
ISBN 0-688-05855-8
ISBN 0-688-05856-6 (lib. bdg.)

Stars are huge balls of hot, glowing gases. Our sun is a star. It is just an ordinary star, not the biggest nor the brightest. But the sun is the star that is nearest to our planet Earth. Earth is part of the sun's family of planets, moons, and comets called the Solar System. All of the other stars that we see in the sky are much farther away from Earth. The stars are so far away from us that even through powerful telescopes they look like small points of light.

People long ago gave names to the brighter stars and learned where and when to look for them. They also gave names to the constellations, groups of stars that seem to form patterns in the sky. Usually these constellations were named after gods, heroes, or animals.

The photograph shows the constellation of Orion, the Hunter. Orion is visible during winter evenings. Look for the three bright stars in a row that form the belt of Orion. The bright red star in the upper left of Orion is named Betelgeuse (most people call it "beetle juice"). The brilliant blue-white star in the lower right is named Rigel. The brightest star in the sky is Sirius, the Dog Star. It is just to the lower left of Orion in the constellation of Canis Major, the Big Dog.

Thousands of years ago Orion looked different then it does today. And thousands of years in the future it will look different than it does now. That's because stars move in space. They move very rapidly, ten or more miles per second. But the stars are so far away from us that we do not notice their motion in our lifetimes.

Imagine traveling in a spaceship going ten miles a second. Even at that speed, it would still take you about three and a half months to reach the sun. But it would take more than seventy thousand *years* to reach the next nearest star, Alpha Centauri.

Alpha Centauri is about twenty-five trillion miles away. There are other stars *millions* of trillions of miles away. These numbers are so big that they are hard to understand. Measuring the distance between the stars in miles is like measuring the distance around the world in inches.

Because of the great distances between stars, scientists measure with the light-year instead of the mile. Light travels at a speed of about 186,000 miles every second. A light-year is the distance that light travels in one year: a bit less than six trillion miles. Alpha Centauri is a little more than four light-years away. The stars shown in this giant cloud of gas in the constellation of Orion are fifteen hundred light-years away.

How many stars do you think you can see on a clear, dark night? Can you see thousands, millions, countless numbers? You may be surprised that in most places only about two thousand stars are visible without a telescope.

When the great scientist Galileo looked through his low-power telescope in the year 1610, he saw thousands and thousands of stars that no one on Earth had ever seen before. As more powerful telescopes were made, millions and millions of other stars were seen.

What looks like clouds in this photograph are really millions of stars too far away to be seen as separate points of light. With powerful telescopes we can see that the stars are as many as the grains of sand on an ocean beach.

Some of the millions and millions of stars in the Milky Way.

Stars are born in giant clouds of gas and dust called nebulas. Most of the gas is hydrogen with a small amount of helium. Over millions of years, gravity pulls the gas and dust particles together and squeezes them so that they heat up. When the gas gets hot enough, it sets off a nuclear reaction like that of a super hydrogen bomb and a star is born. This computer-colored photograph shows a newborn star (*arrow*) in the cloud of gas and dust known as Barnard 5.

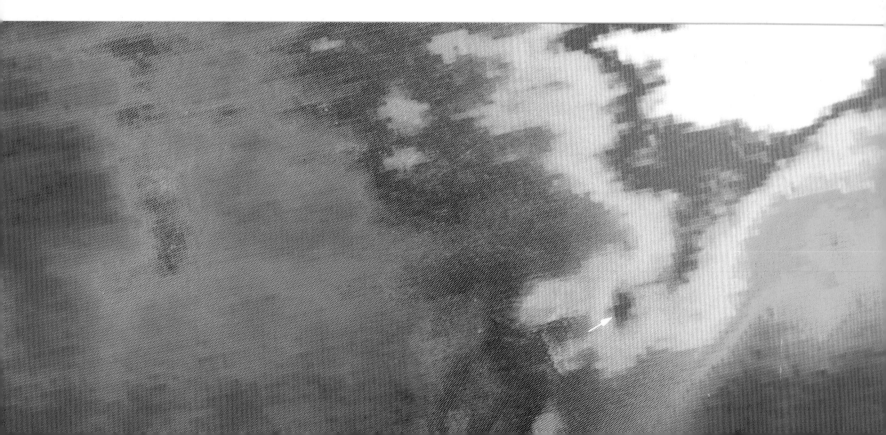

Stars change as they grow older. For example, young stars (10 to 200 million years old) are very hot — with surface temperatures of more than 12,000 degrees (F) — and are usually blue or blue-white in color. Middle-aged stars like our sun are yellow and not as hot — 10,000 degrees (F).

After about ten billion years stars begin to run out of their hydrogen fuel. Most of these old stars collapse upon themselves and they get hotter and hotter. Then, like a piece of popcorn when it "pops," the stars balloon out and become hundreds of times larger. They become what are known as red giant stars.

A red giant star may be 40 or 50 million miles across. Some are even larger. Betelgeuse is a red supergiant star 250 million miles across. If Betelgeuse were put in place of our sun in the center of the Solar System, it would swallow up Mercury, Venus, Earth, and Mars.

Some older stars go through a stage where they keep growing and then shrinking. These stars are called variable stars because at times they appear bright and at other times they are dim.

Other older stars shoot out a large cloud of gas into space. These stars are called planetary nebulas because through low-power telescopes they look like round planets. This photograph taken with a high-power telescope shows the real nature of a planetary nebula. This is the Ring Nebula in the constellation Lyra.

Finally, older stars cool and start collapsing. They shrink down to about the size of a small planet and are called white dwarf stars. As the white dwarfs slowly cool off they become black dwarf stars. And then the stars are dead.

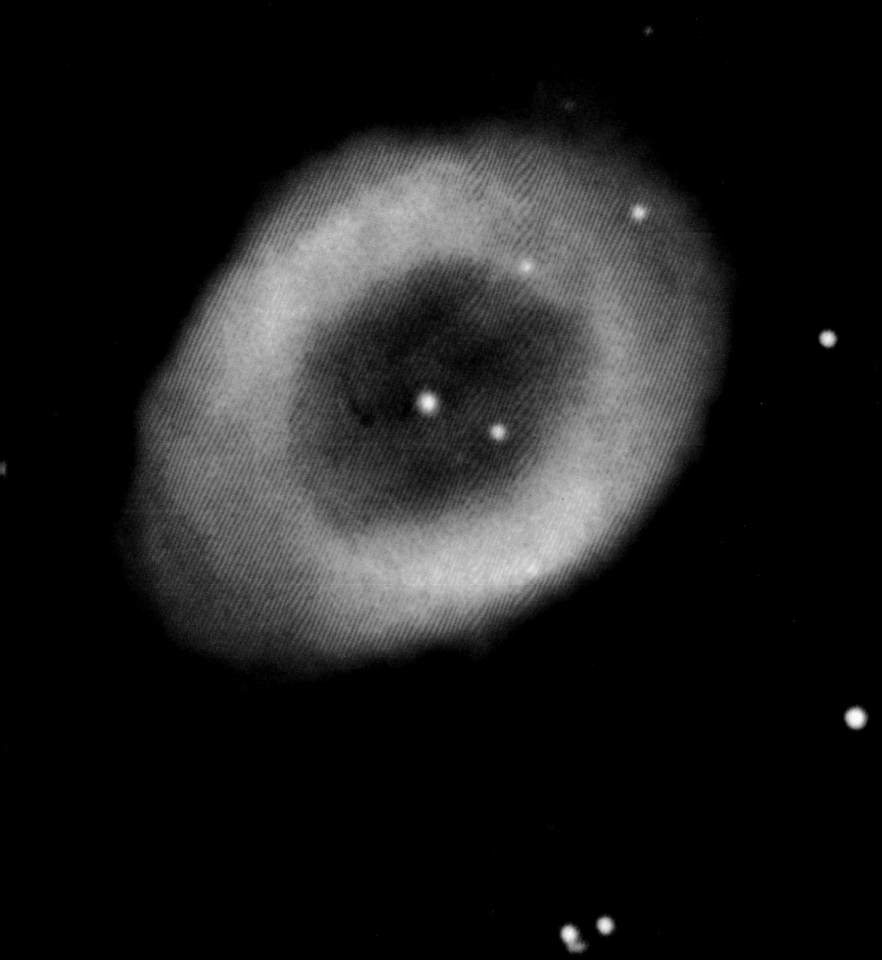

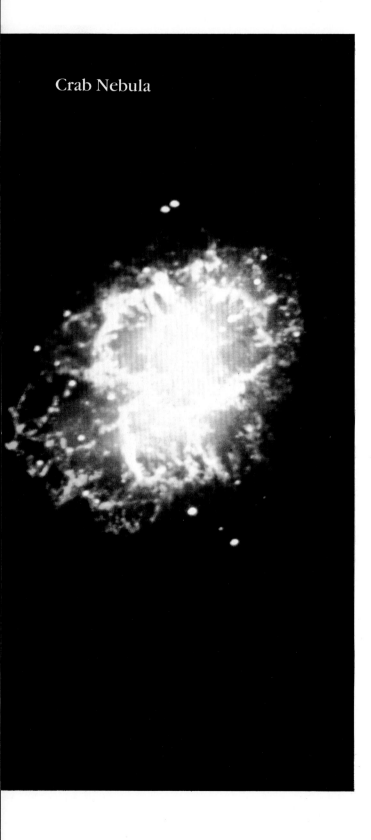

Crab Nebula

Sometimes a star, usually a white dwarf, suddenly explodes and becomes much brighter. To people long ago it looked like a new bright star had appeared in the sky. They called the star a nova (*nova* means "new"). Even though most novas are too far away for us to see, scientists think that two or three dozen novas appear in the Milky Way every year.

Much rarer are the gigantic explosions known as supernovas. A supernova star flares up and becomes millions of times brighter than normal.

A supernova may appear only once every few hundred years. In the year 1054, Chinese astronomers saw a supernova in the constellation of Taurus. Today we can see the gaseous remains of that exploding star. We call it the Crab Nebula.

Some supernovas shatter completely, leaving behind only the wispy gases of a nebula. But a few supernovas leave a small, tightly packed ball of particles called a neutron star. A tiny drop of a neutron star would weigh a billion tons on Earth.

The sudden collapse of a supernova causes a neutron star to spin very rapidly and give off a beam of X-ray radiation. Like the beam from a lighthouse, we can detect the X rays as a pulse. So a rotating neutron star is called a pulsar.

This X-ray photograph shows a pulsar in the middle of the Crab Nebula. The X rays from the pulsar in the Crab blink on and off thirty times every second. The star is visible when the X rays are "on" and invisible when the X rays are "off."

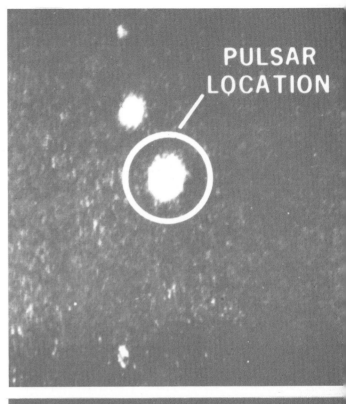

PULSAR LOCATION

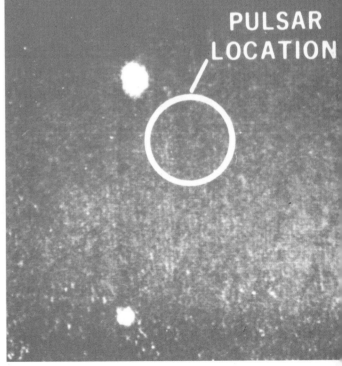

PULSAR LOCATION

Some stars are much larger than the average star. When such a massive star cools and collapses, it becomes something very special. The star is crushed together by the huge weight of the collapsing gases. Gravity keeps squeezing and squeezing until the star seems to disappear. The star has become a black hole.

Anything passing too close to a black hole will be pulled into it and never get out again. Even light is pulled in and cannot escape, so a black hole is invisible. Yet, scientists think they have located several black holes.

This drawing is of a double star called Cygnus X-1. Only one of the stars is visible: a hot, blue giant star. Near it is a black hole that pulls gases from its neighbor. As the gases are sucked in they become so hot that they give off huge amounts of X rays. Some scientists think that there are many such black holes scattered throughout space.

Our sun is an unusual star. It does not have any nearby stars circling it. Most stars have one or more companion stars and they revolve around each other. The star groups are so far from us that most look like single points of light to our eyes.

About half of all the stars we can see are double, or binary, stars. There are also many groups with three, four, a dozen, or even more stars in them. These groups of stars move through space together like flocks of birds in flight. Scientists think that the stars in such a group were all formed at the same time.

Very large groups of stars are called star clusters. This is a photograph of the Pleiades, an open cluster of stars. It contains several hundred stars that form a loose group with no special shape. These are young stars and they are surrounded by clouds of gas and dust.

Here is a different kind of star cluster called a globular cluster. A globular cluster contains many thousands, or even millions, of stars very close together.

This is the great globular cluster known as M.13 in the constellation of Hercules. It is visible just as a dot of light to the naked eye. But through a telescope we can see that it has at least a million stars. Most of these stars are very old and they have stayed together throughout their lifetime.

The biggest star clusters of all are called galaxies. Galaxies are the largest kind of star systems. Our sun and its planets are a member of a galaxy called the Milky Way. There are more than one hundred billion stars in the Milky Way galaxy.

The sun is located almost out on the edges of the Milky Way. All the stars in the Milky Way whirl around the center of the galaxy, each at its own speed. The sun along with the Solar System moves at about 150 miles a second around the center of the galaxy. But the galaxy is so big that the sun takes about 225 million years to go around once.

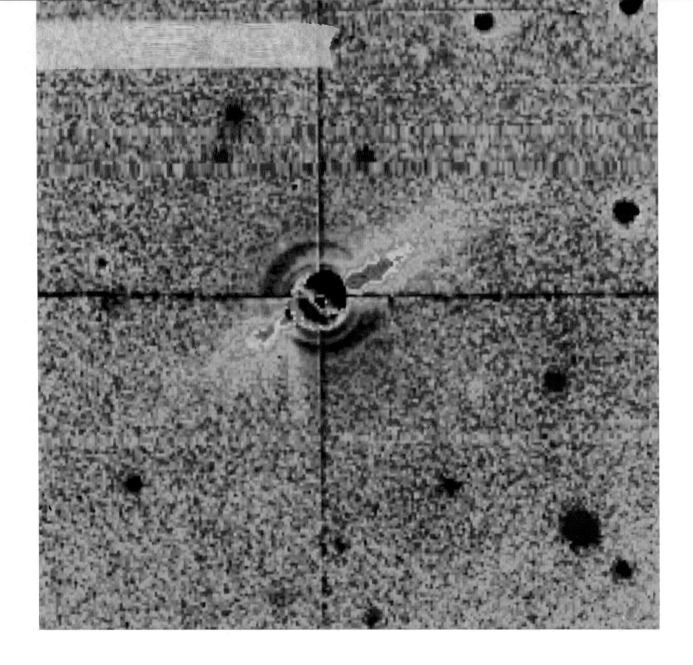

Are there planets circling other stars in our galaxy? The answer is almost definitely yes. This picture shows a ring of material surrounding the star Beta Pictoris. This material is thought to be a young solar system in the making.

Planets form at the same time and from the same gases as do stars. So scientists think it is likely that some or even many stars have planets circling them. If even a tiny percentage of these planets are similar to Earth, then there may be millions of Earth-like planets in the galaxy.

Do any of these planets have life on them? No one knows. But scientists are using radio telescopes to listen for signals of intelligent life in outer space. They think the signals will come in the form of radio waves much like those of our own radios and televisions. So far scientists have not found anything, but they are not discouraged. Until they have examined every star that may have planets they won't know for sure.

The Milky Way is only one galaxy among millions of others in the universe. Galaxies — large and small, single or in groups and clusters, and in many different shapes — are found in every direction.

The Andromeda galaxy, shown here, is a spiral galaxy with almost twice as many stars as there are in the Milky Way. The Andromeda galaxy lies in far distant space, almost twelve quintillion miles away. That's 12,000,000,000,000,000,000! Light from this galaxy has been traveling for more than two million years by the time we see it in our telescopes.

How many galaxies are there in the universe? No one knows. But scientists think that there are about one hundred billion other galaxies. And each one of these galaxies contains hundreds of thousands of mil-

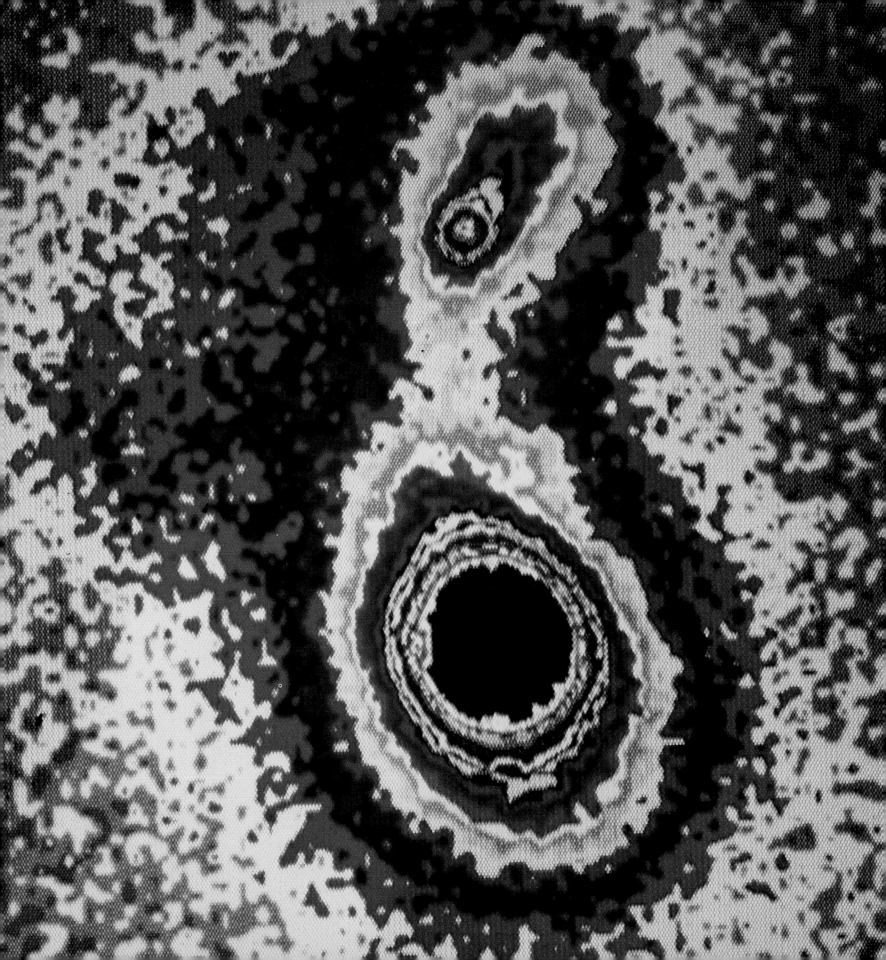

Many mysteries confront us in the distant reaches of space. Beyond most of the galaxies that we can see with our largest telescopes are bright starlike objects called quasars. Each quasar gives off more than one hundred times the energy of all the stars in the Milky Way galaxy put together.

This is a computer-colored photo of a quasar-galaxy pair. Scientists think that quasars may be the centers of young galaxies that are just forming. Light from most quasars has been traveling for ten to fifteen billion years by the time it reaches Earth. That means that we are viewing quasars as they were ten to fifteen billion years ago, just after the universe began.

This photograph of Betelgeuse is the first ever to show the surface of a star other than the sun. Powerful telescopes orbiting above Earth's atmosphere may soon show us the very edges of the universe and the beginning of time itself. Will all our questions about stars then be answered? It's not likely. Each mystery that we solve about space seems to lead to many more unsolved questions about the nature of the universe.

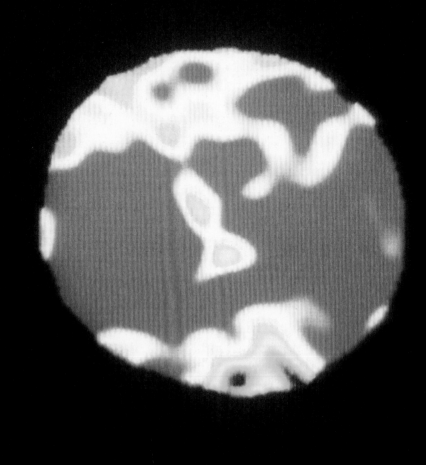